Thank you to my husband for always pushing me to be better, which allows me to help more animals.

7 Miracle Steps to Get Your Dog to Obey:

even if they've failed before

By

Jessica L. Fisher

Jessica L. Fisher, The Furry Family Coach
San Diego, CA

Printed in the United States of America

Jessica L. Fisher, The Furry Family Coach
San Diego, CA

Contents

Jessica L. Fisher

Introduction

Hello and welcome.

I'm Jessica Fisher and I'd like to welcome you to our furry family. In this book we will be talking about how to train your dog. Training your dog actually isn't so much training your dog as it is training *you* to train your dog. Dogs respond to positive behavior modification, not abusive owners. You have to be able to use rewards to help your dog modify behaviors and help show your dog the behaviors you want. But many people go too far and think they need to overwhelm their dog. There is a difference between your dog recognizing you as a loving and caring leader, and an abusive domineering oppressor. No dog, or human, wants to be oppressed and both will always act out in rebellion.

First let's identify some of the problem areas you might be experiencing. These are common pet issues.

1. Aggression Towards Other Pets
2. Food Aggression
3. Misbehaved on a Leash
4. Anxiety When You Leave
5. Dog That **Steals** Things?
6. Jumping Up On Other People
7. Jumping Up On You
8. Digging In Your Yard
9. Not Coming To You When You Call
10. Chewing On Things

11. House Training Issues
12. Biting You
13. Biting Other People
14. Whining When Left Alone
15. Ignoring You
16. Aggression Towards You
17. Aggression Towards Other Dogs
18. Aggression Towards Strangers
19. Aggression Towards Objects
20. Aggression Towards Other Animals
21. Barking At The Door
22. Barking At the Doorbell
23. Running Away
24. Barking When On Walks
25. Chasing Cars
26. Fear of Loud Noises
27. Scratching At Doorways
28. Barking While In The Car
29. Barking When Left Alone
30. Hyperactivity
31. Excessive Licking or Chewing
32. Eating Poop (Coprophagia)
33. Following You To Get Attention
34. Submissive Urination When You Get Home
35. Tail Chasing
36. Jumping Up On Your Furniture
37. A Fear of Objects
38. A Fear of Other People or Dogs
39. Issues with Running Away
40. Unique and Unexplained Behaviors

I know the frustration you feel and how you may feel that nothing really works for your furry little friend, but I assure you, there is hope. I will reveal to you the positive techniques I have taught to thousands of people who now have the quality time with their pets that they never thought would happen.

I want to share with you the secrets of training your furry friend so that you can have more quality time together. No more wasting your money and time on techniques that don't get results.

Before we start in I'd like to tell you a little about myself and introduce the course to you. I became a dog trainer out of the love of animals. I have always loved animals. I started in my early twenties rescuing cats and doing TNR (trap neuter return) in my community and over the years I've evolved to bringing dogs into my home and now I use positive reinforcement to train dogs and help make sure that dogs stay in their forever homes and out of shelters.

My dog's name is Kim. I like to call her my blonde bombshell because that's what she is. She's a gorgeous little blonde bombshell, she loves to do all kinds of things, even chase a lizard through the mulch.

How I trained her, and hundreds of other dogs, is what I'm going to teach you. What you're going to learn is 100% positive reinforcement methods, and we're going to start basically with what I call my Canine Commandments.

Dog Training

The commandments are on the very last page of this book so you can print it out and put it on your refrigerator. I want you to be able to look at it and read it every single day. These are things you're going to want to practice with your dog every day. You will also notice that these are things that will benefit you in other areas of your life also. These are going to be the foundation for all of our training.

I have been in love with animals my entire life, but it was just a few years ago that something happened in my life that led me down the path of becoming a dog trainer. I wish I could say that my lifelong goal, everything I've ever wanted to be since I was a little kid, was a dog trainer, but that really isn't the truth.

What happened to me that set me on this path of becoming a dog trainer? Well, I met someone who I became friends with through Facebook. I had just moved to a new city, in a new state across the country from where I'd been living. Wouldn't you know it, they had dogs.

I always knew I wanted to do something with animals, and during most of my 20s I couldn't figure out any way to work with animals and make money because we all have bills to pay, but I did a lot of charity work, I helped dog rescues, I volunteered, and I still do a lot of that. I've always had a very deep love and empathy with animals, so much so that I even studied animal psychology in college. I graduated from Old Dominion University with a Bachelor's of Science in Psychology.

One of the things I did immediately was to study animal training courses and watch many different trainers over the years. I came to the conclusion that positive training methods are the only training methods that we should use because they are the only humane methods of training. They are also the only methods that get the results we want, not just short term, but also long term. So positive training is what I do.

What does that mean? It means that we use absolutely no fear and no pain. We use rewards to guide and shape our dogs into the dogs we want them to be, and the behaviors we want them to exhibit, the actions we want them to take.

So that really is what you're going to be learning about in this book and it is the same things I teach in my online vídeo training.

My friend had a page for their dogs on Facebook, and I was able to meet and become friends with one of her dogs. Dogs make wonderful friends, but you probably already know that. I loved my new furry friend. I petted her all the time, and we played whenever I could see her. The other dog my friend really never let anybody meet, but one day her female dog I was friends with went to the vet to have surgery to have a cancerous tumor removed. At this point I had not studied any kind of dog training even though I had dogs of my own.

Dog Training

My friend was really anxious, really nervous for her dog to be going to the vet to undergo anesthesia to have this cancerous tumor removed, as anyone one would be, right? Because one, your dog is undergoing anesthesia and, two, you have no idea if the cancer has spread, if they're going to be able to get it all, what the prognosis is going to be after this surgery, so to kind of ease her mind a little bit, I suggested that we take the day, go shopping, and then we would go pick her dog up later from the vet and get her all settled back at her house.

I went over to her house and everything was normal and according to our plans. We were getting ready to leave and she said, "Hey, why don't, since my female dog isn't here, why don't you meet my male dog and give them a treat and kind of get acquainted with him." I'm not using names for privacy.

I was really excited because I never met him before and I wanted to. I really knew almost nothing about him other than he was a rescue dog and had been treated very poorly. We don't know what happened to him before she adopted him. But he was very photogenic and was an amazing subject. The two dogs were brother and sister and really got along well and were very close. That's all I knew about him.

We were in her kitchen and she lets him out. She picks up some treats and hands me one and before I know it her dog leaps up and grabs ahold of her arm and doesn't let go. He really had a strong hold of her arm. I'd never seen a dog attack a person and it seemed like hours, but it was probably 25 to 30 seconds.

Suddenly my mind starts racing, what do I do? What do I do? I need to do something in this situation, this large 90-100 pound dog has ahold of my friend's arm. Quickly I looked around and I saw on the counter there was a bread container, one of those kind of older bread containers where you would sit it on the counter and has that roll top in the front.

I started slamming the door up and down, slamming it onto the counter trying to get his attention. It worked, he let go, looked at the counter where I was making all the noise, and then quickly looked up at me because I was the one making all the noise. Well, I still had a treat in my hand, so he let go of my friend, turned around, and started to lunge at me. I was paying enough attention that I saw him coming and I tried to get out of his way. He nipped at my arm but only barely.

He didn't really get ahold if it, he just kind of scraped me. I have a couple small scars from where he got my arm, and from there, it was just like what to do now? My friend was bleeding profusely. I grabbed a couple of kitchen towels, and started to wrap up her arm. She's yelling at her dog to get in the other room, the dog goes in the other room, she closes the door and is screaming in pain. I'm like, "We've got to get you to the hospital."

We ran to the car and I took her to the hospital.

Well, long story short, it turns out that this dog, they think was being trained possibly to be used in dog fighting before she adopted him. Now, that doesn't mean that he can't be rehabilitated because I firmly believe these dogs can be rehabilitated, and there is proof. In fact, I'm not going to go too much into it, but there is proof.

There are dogs from dog fighting rings who have been rehabilitated and are very loving, adjusted pets afterwards. However, I also found out that she did not know how to handle him. She sent him off to a boot camp for two weeks where they used fear, force, and pain in the form of shock collars as well as physical abuse to train him. She even went so far as to tell me that the trainer she hired to train her dog had been charged with killing dogs by strangling them in his training. Even more of a long story, I knew that I had to learn what happened in those few seconds because he gave signals, and we both should have known what was about to happen.

I can't control the fact that my friend didn't tell me any of this beforehand. She didn't tell me that he had already bitten her twice. She didn't tell me that he had food aggression. She didn't tell me that she was scared of him. She didn't tell me any of these things, and I can't control that, but what I can control is knowing how to identify the body language and the stress signals in a dog to deescalate and avoid these situations, so ultimately that experience is what led me down the path of becoming a dog trainer.

I know that aggressive dogs can be trained because I work with aggression cases. Primarily I work with basic obedience because my whole goal is to make sure that pets stay in loving homes. There are far too many dogs and cats that are relinquished to shelters every year, millions of them, and millions of them are euthanized every single year simply because there's some small issue that the owner can't figure out. I really like to tell people 100% of the time, your dog is doing the absolute best he or she can with the information that you're providing to them. We need to control the pet population by spaying and neutering, not by euthanizing them. That is one of my principle goals in this book, and in what I do.

The first goal I want to teach you is how to speak to your dog in a way that they understand and to teach you how to understand what they are trying to say to you. It is a foreign language to both of you, but once each of you learn the other's language, you can communicate better with your dog and live a very happy life together.

A dog most often becomes a member of your family under the right circumstances. That's how they should be treated. They have a lot of love to give and will accept a lot of love. They always give more than they receive. They can be your best friend, but also a life saver in many ways.

With that, we're going to get into the topic of this book. Thank you so much for reading my story about how I became a dog trainer. I really hope it inspires you to learn more about your dog and what kind of relationship you can have. If you do, you will find that it is a very rewarding relationship.

Dog Training

CHAPTER 1

POSITIVITY

In this chapter we begin talking about our Canine Commandments. I recommend that you read over them carefully and then commit them to memory. Some people put them up on their refrigerator, or on a door, or kitchen cabinet to keep reminding them. Everyone in the house needs to read it over and then post it on a family message board or other place you might have in your home where everybody is going to be able to see it on a daily basis. This is because this is the foundation to all of your dog training.

The first Canine Commandment is positivity. As a positive methods dog trainer, I use positivity all the time working with dogs, and owners. But this is a little bit different. The positivity we're talking about in the canine commandments means that you use positive reinforcement to shape and mold behaviors and actions.

Your dog will respond to this every time. Dogs in this way aren't a lot different than people. There is an old saying, "Treat someone like you'd like them to be and they will become such, treat them like they are, and they will remain the same." A dog responds to this saying very well. Treat a dog that is acting out with negativity and they will continue to act out. Treat them in positive ways and they will conform to how they are treated.

Dog Training

Children do not respond well in life to fear or pain. Spanking has been proven to be counterproductive in all studies regarding children and discipline. It is my experience and the experience of many other experts that dogs similarly do not respond well to fear or pain. Actually, the opposite. When a dog shows up at a rescue center, love and acceptance brings them out of their shell, or their bad behaviors, not more pain and fear.

To maintain an environment where there is no fear or pain, we don't force a dog to do anything. We are shaping their actions and behaviors, or molding them, by giving them a reward, whether that be food, treats, or toys, and much of the time with a lot of praise and affection. We're giving them a reward, positive reinforcement, for what they do right.

So that's basically in a nutshell what Positive Methods Training means. For short, Positivity, as I refer to it in the Canine Commandments. I've trademarked these so if you hear them from other trainers you will know where they got the ideas. The methods I use I give out to all of my in-home customers, and now to you in this booklet.

The Canine Commandments are a basis and foundation for training that you and everyone in your household needs to implement to begin the training process in your home with your dog, or dogs if you have more than one.

With positivity you use a cheerful, happy, and most importantly calm demeanor in your home all the time, and especially when training your dog. Positivity will be incredibly beneficial to you as a person in your life in general if you implement it throughout your whole life. By doing so it will make having a dog easier and more enjoyable, as well as make it easier and stress free in training your dog.

To begin implementing Positivity we create a certain cue connected to a certain behavior that we want them to do or to stop doing. I'm sure you've heard of Pavlov's dog experiments in Russia.

Ivan Petrovich Pavlov was a Russian physiologist known primarily for his work in classical conditioning and worked extensively with dogs. Pavlov won the Nobel Prize for Psychology or Medicine in 1904. He has become one of the top 25 psychologists quoted in the 20th century. Pavlov's principles of conditioning have been successful with a broad range of species, not just dogs or humans. His techniques worked to even reduce phobias and systematic desensitization. This is very important when working with traumatized dogs such as those coming home as war dogs, police dogs, or abused dogs.

Positivity helps a dog relax, feel secure and confident. It helps them be reassured that their surroundings are safe and non-threatening. This is a key in the animal world as their senses are very keen on this aspect of their lives. Humans take it more for granted, but not dogs. They can hear you coming a long way away and their senses are saying to them friend or foe, safe or threat. Humans aren't that keen and we wait to open the door when someone knocks on it before our senses kick in.

Dogs are well known to sense many things humans can't including cancer, kidney stones, and other diseases afflicting humans. Now you can see why a lifetime of training for your dog is so important. Some dogs have attained a vocabulary of hundreds of words that include colors and names of objects, gestures, and hand motions.

More than one person has trained their dog to fetch the evening newspaper, or their slippers, without chewing them to pieces. They are smart and if we can implement positivity in our lives and transfer it to theirs it becomes the foundation for their safe and secure learning environment.

What we invest in our dog and their development we will get back many fold. I really, truly believe what we put into something is what we get back out of it. I'm sure you've heard the phrase, "as ye sow so shall ye reap."

Being positive, being happy, being calm, especially with our dog, is really going to be key here, that's what we're going to get back out of our dog.

This is something that's really going to speak to you if you have a hyperactive dog or a puppy, because we tend to react to everything in life, but, also, with our dog. We react to their actions and behaviors, and reacting is not what we want to do with our dog in general, but especially when training. We want to set an example and be a leader for our dog, very much in the same sense that you are a leader to your children.

Dogs are part of our family even if we don't realize it. They have a family pack, they are born in a litter and that is all they know. Their mentality is similar to ours as families go. You and your family become their family. They seek to fit into the family just as much as they would if they lived in the wild and were introduced into a family of dogs. They all find their place in the social structure of the pack family.

You need to learn how to integrate them into what they view as their new pack family. They live as family units in the wild. If you ever get a chance to look into and study what we know about wild dogs you will see a very specific ordered social structure based around the family. We call their family life a pack. We didn't know much about their family social life until the last 20 and 30 years. Unfortunately, we thought we knew, but the scientific studies that old trainers used, which is where a lot of the dominance and "pack theory" methods came from, was very, very flawed. The researchers who did these studies have even come out against those studies, because of how flawed they were. They are completely inaccurate.

Fortunately, we do know now that dogs in the wild live very much like we do with our children. There's a mother. There's a father, and there are their offspring, and they live as a family unit, and this is exactly how your dogs fit into your home as well. They are part of the family. They need a leader, a mother figure, a father figure, whatever you may be, if you're male or female, to guide them, mold them and shape them into the dog you want them to be, and how they're going to fit into your family, and into your household. So calmness and positivity are going to go a really long way. That is what they are looking for in the wild from their mother and father figure, and they transfer that to you.

Please review the Canine Commandments at the end of the book, then come back and we'll talk about Patience with   your   dog.

Jessica L. Fisher

CHAPTER 2

PATIENCE

In chapter two we are going to talk about our second Canine Commandment, which is Patience. Now, this is going to work kind of into the whole positivity thing, but I find more people have a problem with patience than they do with staying positive. And, I think that's saying something. But, it is incredibly important that we practice patience, especially during our training sessions with our dogs, but really in general with our dogs.

Our dogs are doing the best they can with the information we are providing them. So, if you are getting frustrated and your dog isn't doing what you want them to do, or you expect them to be doing something differently, it's because we haven't given them the proper information to make those decisions on their own yet.

Remember some dogs learn a vocabulary of hundreds of words. It is estimated that the average dog attains a vocabulary of 165 words. Smart dogs do better, over 250. They have their own language and own vocabulary. You have to teach them a new language, human speak. Imagine if you had to learn a dogs language and vocabulary how hard that would be. Think of a new born child how long it takes them to utter their first word, momma, or dadda. When do they say their first sentence? It takes a long time. You are patient with your child, you can be patient with your dog.

Patience needs to be practiced, because, they really are trying to do exactly what we want them to do. Remember the pack family, well they are trying to fit into a new family unit, their new pack family. It is their instinct to fit in and be a part, they want to, they need to fit in. So, they are trying. However, they're only able to do what they know how to do, so if you haven't yet trained them, shaped them, molded them in their behavior or their action into what you expect them to do, then really, it's your own fault that they're not doing it right.

So, we need to practice patience.

For example, I was working with a young lady and her German Shepherd not too long ago. Her name is Abby and her dog's name is Chico. Abby was trying to do all the right things, use positive reinforcement to shape behaviors in Chico, but her patience level was so incredibly low the only thing happening was frustration … on both parts.

She'd work on a cue, for example sit, and although Chico was getting the hang of it, she couldn't wait for him to stay in the sit position longer than a second and simply got frustrated when he had realized that all it took was his bottom on the floor to get the treat. There was no longevity to the sit and Abby couldn't understand why Chico wouldn't just stay sitting.

It didn't take long, maybe 15 minutes, working with Chico to get him to remain in a sitting position for a period of time. He was a bright dog, but Abby simply didn't have the patience needed to help Chico learn what she actually wanted.

After spending a few minutes with Chico and showing Abby what he could do, I turned my training hat to her. Chico is the easy part … Abby is the other piece of the puzzle that most dog trainers overlook.

If they don't get it right the first time, then try again and maybe you need to adjust the way you're teaching. But that's what the whole course is about, right? I teach you methods and techniques. In the online dog training course, as soon as we're done with the Canine Commandments we start getting into a lot of the different cues you can teach your dog, and then molding and shaping certain behaviors out of your dog or into your dog, depending on what those behaviors may be, whether you want them to do something or whether you want them to stop doing something.

We then get into how to mold and shape those behaviors. But, it's okay if they don't get it the very first time. You didn't walk the first time you tried, right? You didn't crawl the first time you tried. You didn't swim properly the first time you tried. So the first time you start to train a cue or train a behavior modification, you may not get to the point you want to get to, and that's okay because what we want to do 100% of the time is end on a positive note. So, if you're frustrated or if your dog is frustrated, you need to stop and take a break.

No one rides a bike the first time they try, not even adults. As we train, the steps are to introduce the dog to what we want them to do, and give them an opportunity to do it. And if it doesn't go right, we try again, then again, and if there is failure that is okay, always end on a positive note. No scolding, no bad words, no shaking fingers, no harsh words.

Patience, affection, and love. "That's alright Trooper we will try again tomorrow." Sounds like teaching a child something? Of course it is, just like teaching a child. Dogs have the mental ability and capacity of about a two year old, so think of it in those terms. Some of the smarter dogs attain the mental ability of a two and a half year old, but can do math at a three or four year old level. But, their social skills are off the charts next to children. Their pack instincts bring something to the table that humans don't have. We need to learn that and how to take advantage of it.

Go back to the last step that your dog did complete successfully. Even if that's just to sit or to lie down or be quiet. Whatever it may be, something you know your dog can do. At that point, give them positive reinforcement. First your approval and praise, then afterwards your affection, petting works, they like to be touched. Perhaps giving them a smile so they know the expression on your face says love and approval. Dogs have looks, so do humans, and they can pick up on yours very easily.

I use my facial expressions every single day with my dog. And, my dog has learned to give back a facial expression telling me things. I try to get my dog to express itself on a daily basis. I ask for it daily because I want to reinforce it.

Through a positive note ending in any training session it helps with reinforcement, bonding, and helping our dog know where it is in the pack family. Another animal that is very pack oriented I'm sure you know about is Lions. You've seen the lioness let the cubs play all over her and jump on her, bite her ear, pull her tail and then suddenly, but gently, she whacks one with a paw. All the rest of the cubs look around and get the message. There are boundaries.

Dogs are the same. They need to know their boundaries and in the wild dogs teach this to each other. As the mother or father of the family, you need to teach it too in a similar patient, gentle way. If you're frustrated, if your dog is frustrated, it builds a wall. So stop, go back to something, either the last step they completed successfully or something else you know they already know how to do. Get them to do that. Give them a treat. Give them lots of praise. End on a positive note, because that's what's going to remain in your dog's mind.

It's also what's going to remain in your mind. So, if you end frustrated, if you just stop because your dog isn't doing what you want them to do and you can't figure something out, or you have anxiety or you're frustrated, or whatever it is you may feel, if you end that way, that's how you're going to start the next session. And, we never want to do that.

Another thought is expectations. If your dog expects they will fail, they will. If they expect to pee on the carpet anywhere because you let them, they will. How can you be frustrated at that if you let them do it? If you expect it and don't do anything about it, the dog will fail at potty training.

Being positive creates a happy, self-confident and secure dog. Ending on a downer creates an insecure and self-conscious dog. Which do you want? Ending on them doing something the way you want them to do it builds on future training exercises.

I advise ending by giving them a treat, along with giving them praise. End on you being happy with what they've done. That's what your dog needs from you.

Dog Training

CHAPTER 3

SHAPING YOUR DOGS BEHAVIOR

All right. So, let's talk some more about our Canine Commandments.

Our next one is, "Shaping your dog's behavior." By now you probably understand what I'm talking about because I've talked about it a little bit already.

With positive reinforcement, what we're doing is we're using high value rewards, and in the beginning, for most dogs, this is going to be a yummy treat. For other dogs, it could be toys or playtime. For all dogs, we're also going to use love and praise. So, these are high value rewards that we are giving to our dogs when they perform an action or behavior that we want them to do.

This is really the basis for positive methods training. It's exactly what positive reinforcement is. They do X, we give them a high value reward for doing that. And this is how we use positive reinforcement to shape and mold behaviors in our dogs.

For example, when we get to some of the cues, when we want our dog to look at us, we're going to show a little treat, let them smell it, then we bring it up close to our eye and as soon as their eye makes contact with us, we give them the treat. You can tell. Their eye is making contact with your eye. You're going to say the word, "Look!" And then, "Yes!"

Dog Training

In addition to using a treat you can use a clicker. If you choose to use a clicker it can be cue signaling a reinforcement. Instead of saying the word "look" which is a marker for the behavior you want to acknowledge, you can instead use a clicker to mark that behavior.

You can do the same thing to mark that action and give them the reward, which in this case is going to be a treat. Also reinforce it with praise and touch. A pat on the head, hug, something that gives them the warm and fuzzies.

We mark the behavior with a key word. I like to use the word, "Yes!" Instead of a word you can also use a clicker. We're going to mark that behavior and reward it, and that is how we shape and mold behaviors in our dogs. That's how positive reinforcement works.

So, onto the next Canine Commandment, be the protector. Just a foreword here, many people may be familiar with the term "pack leader" and I want to caution you to be very wary of this old way of thinking. We are a family unit, and yes, we commonly refer to a family of dogs in the wild as a pack, but this in no way should equate to dominance in our minds.

Jessica L. Fisher

CHAPTER 4

BE THE PROTECTOR

All right. So, now we are at, "Be the protector." This is our next Canine Commandment. In this one, we're going to talk a little bit about history.

When humans first decided that wolves were beneficial and we started breeding wolves into dogs to be our companions we treated them a certain way. We took them out of their natural state and placed them in an unnatural state. Dogs react differently in a group than they did as wolves. Wolves are very territorial and family group oriented. A pack of dogs are neither territorial or family group oriented. They have no leader of the pack or Alpha among them.

You don't need to be the dominant Alpha, you need to be the head of the family. The head of the family is the natural protector. Puppies look for momma for protection. When scared they will roll on their back in submission voluntarily.

Kim, my dog, wants to play. Dogs like to play. They like to run and have fun. There are mutual benefits to both you and the dog. When training first began of dogs they were trained as guard dogs to stay awake at night and watch. They have really good hearing, and they could alert humans in a camp or in a group, in a colony, even on ships, to threats coming towards them. The dogs were so valuable their role expanded to day and night, and even personal body guards.

The Egyptians valued them so much they made them gods and created board games to play in honor of dogs. Egyptian rulers, and many others afterwards, always had a dog around them to protect them from being poisoned or being surprised by an assassin. So nighttime alertness was especially important.

In return, we protect our dogs from things that will hurt them, like other predators. Dogs are known to attack cougars, bears, and almost any animal, human or otherwise, to protect their owners.

It is a mutually beneficial relationship. The reason I'm telling you this, and the reason this is important is because we are the protector. A lot of people get this kind of backwards. They think the dog is protecting them. Not true. We are the protector. Not only are we the protector of our territory or our property, we are our dog's protector, because they are part of our family unit, which some may call, "a pack," in the wild. Mother, father, and their offspring, right? They are part of our family. I keep saying that, but you need to understand the nature of what your dog is thinking, not what you think. A dog to you may be a pet, but you to the dog is family. Treat them that way and they will act that way.

The reason why it is important for us to know that we are the protector is because often owners fail to let our dogs know that we are the protector, and this is where a lot of problems start. When a dog understands we are the protector we reduce their fear and their stress. We need to figure out how to let our dog know that it is their job to alert us to danger.

For instance, they need to hear us convey the meaning of, "The UPS driver has pulled up and it is okay for you to bark and let me know that." In fact, any stranger that comes on the property, or to the door, it is okay for them to take action. Maybe not bark, but instead run to the door and sniff or point or sit by it. Maybe it is jump on the couch and look out the window. You can train them to do many things to alert you that you can live with. Many people can't stand their dog barking at everything. It is up to you, that is why we are training the dog and shaping their behavior.

But, ultimately, we have to let our dogs know that once they have alerted us to the danger, which is their job, it is then our decision what action to take. This is what we want them to do. Alert us to potential dangers. Then, it is our responsibility to let our dog know, and this is what people don't know how to do, let our dog know how to then back off because we are the protector.

"Ok, I got this, you can stop now because I am here. I'm aware of the situation, and either the situation is okay or I'm going to take over and protect." That is your message and your dog has to be trained by your expression, key words, or verbally to know what is expected and his proper roll and behavior. And 99 times out of 100, everything's okay and there is nothing to worry about. We don't want a situation where we do have to worry, but that is what our dog is there for, to let us know about impending danger.

So, here is how we're going to do that in my <u>training classes,</u> and I'm going to give you a little sneak peek right now as to how we're going to do this, and then later on, in the behavioral modification section of the course I offer, we can talk about how to stop the barking, because that is what your dog is supposed to do, bark to let you know there is impending danger.

Basically, what we have to do is we have put a protocol in place to let our dog know once they start barking that, "Okay, now, I understand. I'm here. I'm taking over." There are a couple of different ways to do this. The one I like the most and works with most dogs is a few simple words. I like to use the words, "Thank you." You can also use the word, "Friend," or anything else where you use an upbeat tone. Besides their potential vocabulary of between 150-1,000 words, tone is extremely important. They know tone far better than humans because of their range of hearing. They hear things in tone we miss.

When your dog starts barking or alerting, I like to say alerting, at something, say, "Thank you!" And make sure your dog can hear it. Normally they can, but make sure your dog hears you say, "Thank you." You might have to yell it if you're in another room, but say, "Thank you!"

Dogs also like their name. I knew a lady who was sitting on her couch one night in Florida and her dog was very attentive and it seemed like he knew what she was thinking or going to do before she got up and did something. One night she was sitting their thinking about her dog Chester and she had an idea. She yelled "Chester" in her mind, no words, no movement, sitting perfectly still. Chester was laying at her feet. Chester immediately rose up and looked at her, then looked around attentively. He looked back at her as if to say, "What? What did I miss?"

She smiled at him and he laid back down. She still insists dogs hear more than just the spoken word. Or better yet, they sense those emotions that call them to attention.

If your dog does not stop barking and, especially right away, your dog is not going to stop barking, because we have to put this protocol in place. They're not going to automatically know right upfront what you're doing. We have to practice this over and over. They will eventually learn.

Walk to wherever they are alerting at. For example, if it's a window, get in between them and the window.

Your dog is here, the window is there. You get in between your dog and the window with your back to your dog. Calmly, calmly say, "Thank you!" And at this point, this is when we want our dog to stop barking because we have let them know that we have come and assessed the situation that they have brought to our attention and we're letting them know that everything is okay.

Now, initially your dog is not going to know, even at this point, to stop barking, though you're giving them pretty strong body language letting them know that everything is okay. You have never done this with them before, so they're going to still have to learn it from repetition. They will get it that everything is all right by your tone, your body language, and your calmness. They have a wide range of language skills and will pick up yours if you teach it to them.

Then we want to distract them and reward them for being a good watch dog and alerting you and stopping barking. If they immediately stop barking, reward it. Go ahead with a treat, with praise and love, go ahead and reward it. Then we want to get a squeaky toy or something and distract them from whatever was going on. We are in, a sense, letting them know, "Everything's okay. Let's go back to our regular day."

If your dog just cannot stop barking at this point, then we're going to do a little timeout. I'll talk more about that later on, but what you're eventually going to be able to do is say, "Thank you." The first real goal marker here is to be able to stand in front of them, in between them and the perceived threat, and say, "Thank you!" And they will learn to stop barking. That is really going to be the goal and a learned behavior for them. Remember, they won't get it the first time, but with repetition they will. It will happen pretty soon.

Every dog is different as to how long it will take, especially if they've been doing it for years and years and years, right? If they've been barking for years and years and years, then they have learned from you that it is ok to bark all they want. So with your new behavior they may be a bit confused at first. They will be thinking, "That's not how my momma reacts, what's wrong here?" But by showing them it is ok to stop barking they will adapt to their new role, because you're taking over the responsibility. Then, it may take them longer to catch on.

But dogs are smart, okay? They're going to catch on, especially if you carry yourself in an appropriate way that they understand your body language that, "Yep! Everything's okay! Let's go back to what we were doing."

You'll be very happy when this finally happens. But remember, the whole idea here is that you are the protector.

Jessica L. Fisher

CHAPTER 5

EVERYTHING ON YOUR TERMS

In this chapter we're going to be talking about Everything On Your Terms. This one also, a lot of people misunderstand. Everything On Your Terms, what does this mean? This means that you are the leader, you are the head of the household. In another chapter we talked briefly about how dogs in the wild live as a family unit. Dogs in our household are part of our family and we need to be their leader, much like being a parent.

So if we start letting our dogs control our lives, meaning they tell us when it's time to play, they tell us when it's time to eat, they tell us what they want to do, when they want to do it, and where they want to do it, then it's really going to be hard to be their leader and be their parent.

I knew a woman who had a small dog that didn't like to go outside to take care of nature so it would pee anywhere it wanted to all around the house. So everywhere it would pee she put down a plastic pad so if it peed there again the pad would catch it. Pretty soon they were all over the house and you could hardly walk anywhere without stepping on one. Eventually she did two things. One she got training for the dog to pee out side, and two she replaced all the carpets in her house. She should have gotten the dog training earlier it would have saved her a lot of money.

This is what I'm talking about, don't let your dog rule the house and do what it wants, you have to be in control.

It is exactly the same way as it is with your child. If you have a child who tells their parent this is what I want, this is how I want it and you're going to do it now, that child is not going to respect their parent. Nor will they listen to their parent. It's very similar with dogs.

As humans our communication pattern is broader with dogs than it is with other humans. We're using more body language than we are words because dogs don't speak English. So the one thing I really want to stress here is that you have to decide when meal times are, and you decide when play time is, and you decide when it's time to go for a walk. And we don't let our dogs bully us into giving them food, or going for a walk, or playing.

But what's really important to understand here is that our dogs have needs we have to be attuned to. Like a child, we need to be cognizant of their needs for a potty break outside, or water in their bowl, or a warm pad to lay on.

We can't just say, "Oh, I'll take care of them later." They need visits to the vet and shots just like children. If we don't want to take care of a dog we shouldn't have a dog. If we don't take care of them their instincts will kick in and they will try to take care of themselves by reverting to their most primitive nature and that means usurping your position, authority and place in the family. What does that mean? It means your dog will start bullying you into doing these things they want you to do. Does that make sense to you? Of course it does.

So they need play time every day. They need exercise for good health just like you do. We've created an environment for them to adjust to living with us, but their nature is still what God gave them and that hasn't changed. As anyone knows, feral animals revert very quickly to their natural instincts and those most often are not friendly to humans.

They have an instinct for survival, either meet their needs to survive or their instinct will drive them to meet their own needs. So, they need to be walked, and they need physical and mental exercise and stimulation. Of course you need to feed them every day. So if you're not doing these things, I expect your dogs to start bullying you into doing them because they have biological needs.

However, as long as we are doing these things, and we are properly providing them with all of the physical exercise they need, and all of the mental exercise they need, and their proper nutrition, and we are grooming them like we're supposed to, and we are taking care of them the way we're supposed to, then there's no sense in letting our dogs bully us into when they want to do something.

Through your care of them, they are shaped into the behaviors we expect from a civilized dog, and you are able to guide them and mold them and shape them into being a dog that lives well, not only in your household, but in society when you take them out of the house.

So that is essentially what we mean by Everything On Your Terms. If you have any questions about that, please reach out to me, whether it's an email, or in our <u>Facebook group</u>. I maintain a Facebook page and website for people to reach out to me and get more information and be able to take my classes or use my expertise in consulting on how to have a dog that is better behaved.

CHAPTER 6

WALKING BUILDS BONDS

The next Canine Commandment is Walking Builds Bonds. That one should be pretty self-explanatory, but we need to walk with our dogs and, ideally, we want to be loose-leash walking with our dog. We want them to be able to go out and enjoy the world. Our dogs love to just be outside and exploring. There are so many smells and sights and things for them to do. It really is an enrichment activity, but it really gives you a great opportunity to bond with your dog.

So I don't want you to take this part for granted. I really want you to get out there, and even if you only start with three, maybe four days a week. Your dog would love it to go out every single day of the week, but let's start where we can. If you're not already walking your dog, please, let's get out there and do it because it is an amazing chance to bond with your dog. It's a really great way to train with your dog as well.

So there are a couple different kinds of walks and, more often than not, I like my dogs to have a free walk where there's not a whole lot of structure to the walk other than the fact that they are on a leash, but they are free to smell what they want to smell. I mostly direct where we go, but as long as they're not running off and dragging me down a strange alley we're going to go as much in the direction they want to go as much as I possibly can. I love for them get out and have that enrichment.

Then there are really structured walks, where I decide exactly where we're going, how long we're going, when they can and can't smell something. And the reason this is important is because you want to be able to get to that point where you have trained your dog, that even though there's a stimulus there that they want to check out, maybe it's too dangerous so you want to say, "Leave it."

Just like the stop barking, or look me in the eye, or "leave my shoes alone," you have to be able to give a cue and they listen because their judgement isn't as good as your judgement. You can make walks an opportunity to create cues and reinforce key words that adjust their behavior.

So they are a couple of different things we can integrate into a lot of our walks. I say "leave it" and have my dog come back by my side. This is even when we're out having a fun, free walking experience where she can go and smell, do what she wants. Danger is always just around the corner, as they say, right? But please get out and walk with your dog, it's going to be an amazing bonding experience. Just getting out and walking with your dog will build that bond between you and your dog and will make training easier.

Jessica L. Fisher

CHAPTER 7

REMAIN CONSISTENT

This is the final Canine Commandment, Remain Consistent. This is one of the hardest. Just when you think you've got things going good, you let down and training starts to slip. But this is so important. Remain consistent with your behaviors and with the behavior you want to see from your dog. It's also important as, just a side note not just that you are remaining consistent, but that everyone in the household is consistent. An example of this may be when you are training your dog to sit.

When I train dogs to sit, I use my finger pointing down along with the word "sit." Eventually I want to just to be able to do this and have my dog sit without me actually having to say the word "sit." Now, if you're doing this and you're expecting the dog to sit he'll get it sooner or later. But more, when your spouse says sit, the dog will obey that as well. It will be one of the 165 words they learn early on. But, one of the benefits is if your spouse says "Sit," it will work for them also if both of you do it the same way and are consistent.

Your dog is not going to understand doing things differently, so it's important not only for you to remain consistent with sit, or whatever else you may be training with your dog, but also that everyone in the household has a consistency between what you're doing. Decide, each step of the way what hand signal you're going to use, what word you're going to use to cue a behavior.

Do it with all of the training in your home, right? If mom feeds the dog in the morning and dad feeds the dog in the evening, everyone should know that so that your dog doesn't get double fed. There's a consistency that you need to have in your home through everything including training.

There is no exception when it comes to training your dog, you have to remain consistent both with how you train and with what you train, as well as continuing the training.

Consistency doesn't just stop with the signals you're using or the keywords you're using, but also that you need to be training consistently. You can't start training the cue for sit today and stop for three weeks and then expect the dog will remember.

Would you be able to do that if you were, say, two or three years old? Would you remember something from three weeks ago that hasn't been brought up since? Probably not. So remember when we're training our dogs that we want consistency in everything.

CHAPTER 8

YOUR DOGS NEEDS

In this chapter we're going to be talking a little bit about your dog's needs, and as a force free trainer I am always looking for new ways of behavior modification. Not just new ways, but what people in the field are doing, new methods and how we're evolving as dog trainers. A lot of the old methods are just so outdated, they're inhumane. I won't use them, and you don't want to use them, that's why you're reading this, right?

One of the things I'm really proud to use as a force free trainer is The Hierarchy Of Dog's Needs. I'm just going to give you a quick little glimpse right there. Linda Michaels is a leader in the force free training movement that's going on in the United States, and across the world. She is the developer of The Hierarchy Of Dog's Needs, and I really love that we have very similar backgrounds.

Her primary degree is in psychology, and so is mine, so she kind of used a lot of what she learned in human psychology and transformed it into what works for dogs. She builds on Dr. Marc Bekoff, a PhD in Animal Behavior and likes to quote him saying, "Dogs, like us, need to feel safe, at peace and loved. They depend on us to fill these needs and we are obligated to do so." I whole heartedly endorse that quote from Dr. Bekoff.

What Linda has produced is a pyramid that allows you to see the base needs of your dog and moves upward. She starts with at the base biological needs. Then the second layer is emotional needs. Social needs follow that, which is very important as we've talked about. Then she lists force free training. I interpret this as a force free, non-threatening environment. That is critical to every living being canine or human or any other creature. Finally, she lists Cognitive needs. Dogs need to be stimulated with challenges, thinking, and mental problems that they can solve just like humans.

The base is obviously the bulk of what a dog needs. These are your dog's minimum needs of food, water, shelter, sleep, and the basics of survival. Then from there we have emotional needs. Emotional needs of course mean they need to be loved. But it is more than that. It is a sense of belonging, being in a family, their pack, their reality of existence. Humans can provide that and do provide that, if or when done properly. They need to have a sense of security. They need to be able to trust you, and all part of that is the consistency you provide your dog. It's going to provide that basis for trust, and love, and security. The reason why it's one of our Canine Commandments.

Social needs have to do with bonding with people, and other dogs, or other animals if you have a cat in your family. They need to play and be active with interaction with other beings. It creates a social network that all humans depend on. A dog alone soon exhibits the same mental troubles that prisoners in solitary confinement exhibit. Many prisoners go insane and dogs that have been isolated and chained up have serious mental problems.

Having these connections, these interpersonal connections, just like you, are essential for your dog. If you have another dog in the house that's great, if it's just the bond that you share with your dog that's great, but you need to have it. Unfortunately for many years people didn't have these bonds with their dogs that we now know they need, just as much as we need it.

We have such a strong need for the emotional bond of a dog, because it's really in my opinion, and a lot of peoples' opinion sometimes it's the only time we really feel unconditional love in our life. That's okay, I mean a dog isn't a human, but that also gives them the ability to unconditionally love. So, we need to be able to reciprocate that in the best way possible.

The next level of need your dog has is for a threat free existence. Every human, every animal on earth, needs that kind of loving environment to live. We look again at prisoners, POWs, and those in some form of captivity where their existence is threatened, and we see all kinds of mental illnesses. Linda uses the words "force free training," and I subscribe to those. I love that this is included on The Hierarchy of Dogs Needs.

I can't really imagine an instance where a dog would need absolutely no training. Dogs need to be trained, and if you don't like that term then perhaps, socialized. They need to fit into their social setting be it an apartment in Cleveland or a farm in Arizona. If humans don't help them do that, they will do it naturally themselves. They will learn to come when called simply by repetition. They will learn what you call them, whatever it is.

John Wayne in one of his movies had a dog for a companion and called it "dog." The dog knew its name was Dog and responded to it accordingly. There are really important things for dogs to learn for safety of your dog and your safety.

The act of training your dog forms bonds. You are forming trust and bonding with your dog, which also takes care of some of those social needs that your dog has. I love that that's included in The Hierarchy of Dog's Needs. It is the core of how I base all of my training.

Finally, at the very top of the pyramid, is the cognitive needs of your dog. This is something that is more overlooked than anything else among dog owners. They need to be working their brain. They need stimulation. They need to solve problems. In the wild they have to solve problems everyday of their existence. When they live with humans a lot of their problems are already solved for them. They don't have to go out hunting for something to eat or look out for predators looking to make them a meal. They aren't looking for a warm bed, or clean water. So, they sit around and chew on a bone or listen to your TV as you watch the news at night. That doesn't do it.

You may have heard the term Canine Enrichment, it's a term referring to activities that do just this, provide for the cognitive needs of your dog. I use this term regularly, so if you read or hear it, understand that they are activities for cognitive function.

One of the best ways to provide canine enrichment, or cognitive play, for your dog is through nose work. This is where your dog will have to use their nose to sniff something out, be it a tasty treat or another scent you have worked with your dog to detect. Nose work is one of the best ways to get your dog active because it uses both their nose, or olfactory system, and their brains! When I talk to people who use nose work with their dog, even dogs who are trained to sniff out certain scents such as bomb dogs and drug dogs, this activity wears out the dog quickly. They love it! But it does wear them out.

So, if you have a dog with a ton of energy, nose work would be one of my first recommendations.

Another great way to utilize canine enrichment in your dog's life is to not feed your dog from a bowl. If you feed kibble, which I never recommend (a topic for another book, but certainly often spoken about in my blog and in my Facebook group), you can use a number of toys to feed your dog their food. These toys are designed to make your dog use their brains to gain access to the tasty treats inside.

You can also make items to utilize with feeding, such as a snuffle mat. You can see how to make one in my YouTube video: http://bit.ly/snufflematcanine

This is basically a plastic mat with fleece fabric that you "hide" food or treats in for your dog to sniff out.

But canine enrichment doesn't have to be completely revolved around food. In fact, one of the best enrichment activities is to take your dog on a leisurely walk and just let them smell all the smells. To you it's just grass and trees and maybe cars, but to your dog it's a world of thousands, even millions, of different sights and smells. Remember that you get out of the house, you have work, friends, maybe school, family to visit, etc. Your dog doesn't, so every time you take them out of the house is like a field trip to them! Let them enjoy it!

It's going to help them become more confident. It's going to help them burn energy. It's going to help them all around, I mean if we didn't use our brains we would go crazy too. So, having their cognitive needs met is one of the biggest things people tend to overlook, and it's also one of the most powerful things we can do when we're training our dog.

In our training program we look at the behavior of your dog and what you want them to be doing that they aren't. It will take training of both of you. In our training we look for the root cause of what's going on, not just the effect of what is happening. Really what's going on with your dog, we need to figure that out, so we can make sure that your dog's needs are met appropriately.

That way the behavior that you're not liking will be able to subside. We're going to use a lot of root cause analysis to determine application of the appropriate solutions.

Throughout our training program I'm going to be talking about all of the different things both you and your dog need to learn. The methods, tips, tricks and fun things that make owning a dog the rewarding experience it is.

We have a group that is a support group for dog owners and those who are taking advantage of our training program and methods. Feel free to reach out to the group (https://bit.ly/trainpositive) if you have any questions whatsoever. We do need to make sure that all of the needs of our dogs are met.

If these needs aren't met your dog is not going to be their optimal self. If they are, and you've trained them properly, you'll find a greater unconditional love than you've ever found before.

CHAPTER 9

MYTHS ABOUT DOG TRAINING

Myth #1 — Your Dog needs a Shock Collar

A shock collar is a small electrical device that attaches to your dogs' collar around his neck. The idea is that when your dog barks, the device "corrects" your dog by sending a low voltage shock to your dogs' throat. While manufacturers of these devices say they are safe and don't hurt, they really do. They hurt an awful lot. Imagine how your dog feels. It's not only sad but terribly cruel. It truly breaks my heart that these devices are still being sold today. Not only are they terribly painful but they also stress your dog and they won't work on all dogs. Why is this? Because some dogs will simply push through the pain and others will become depressed and remain silent. It's truly sad. Training a dog with pain is flat out cruel and it is not effective long term. There are so many more effective and humane methods that I can show you, so if you have a shock collar throw it out now!

Myth #2 — You Need to Shout and Scream to Make Your Dog Obey and Listen to You

I've spoken with so many people who think they have to be louder than their dog, so their dog hears them, this simply isn't true. In fact, yelling and screaming does the exact OPPOSITE of what you want. It may help at first, but your dog quickly learns to ignore it and you just look like a mean person yelling at their dog.

To really train your dog you must gain their trust and then they choose to follow your direction. It's that simple.

Myth #3 — You Can't Teach Older Dogs New Things

I don't even know where this saying originated, but it has to come from those outdated training methods. It simply isn't true. Not only is it not true, but I actually find older dogs easier to train than younger puppies most of the time. Puppies are easily shaped into happy, well behaved dogs, but older don't have the same energy level that puppies do. This means that you can get the attention of an older dog much easier. You CAN teach old dogs new tricks, if you know how to do it properly. I'll show you how!

Myth #4 — You Must Be Physical With Your Dog

This is just downright WRONG and INHUMANE on top of that! You are not going to gain your dog's respect by making them fear you. The goal is to be a leader your dog trusts and looks to for guidance.

One of the biggest secrets to training a dog is to EARN their respect. Fear does not equal respect. In fact, fear will eventually leave you in a bad situation where your dog turns on you, and you probably deserve it.

I will show you how to earn your dogs' trust and respect which will make training your dog so much easier.

Myth #5 — A Dog Trainer Can Train Your Dog For You

OK so this drives me nuts! It's one of the things I hear more often than I'd like to share. Someone wants training and the first thing they say is "So do I just leave them with you for the day?" How do you expect your dog to change if you don't change? It doesn't work. Think of it this way... if your child acts up in your home, goes to your sisters' home and is a perfect angel do you expect them to come back to you a perfect angel? The answer is no. You have to earn your dogs trust and respect. Then your dog will gladly follow your lead.

Myth #6 — If the Dog Isn't Trainable, it is The Dog's Fault

After all my years of training some of the most difficult and stubborn dogs, of all sizes, shapes and breeds, I've never seen a dog that has something wrong with them that makes them un-trainable.

NOT...ONE...SINGLE...TIME. The problem is never the dog. The real problem is what the trainer or dog owner is doing. This should be great news for any frustrated dog owner who thinks that something is wrong with their dog. This means no more wasting hundreds, if not thousands of dollars, on vet visits or even Prozac for dogs. You can't change a dog's personality, but YOU can train them when you know how. And that's exactly what I'll show you how to do, step-by-step, with my proven methods.

For more dog training, including instructional videos, go to:

https://www.thefurryfamilycoach.com

Canine Commands

1. Positivity - always remain calm and positive with you dog. Your energy determines their behavior. Remain clam and positive and they will too!

2. Patience - You and your dog speak different languages. Be patient, take your time, take breaks, tray again.

3. Shape Your Dogs Behaviors - Use food and other high value objects to shape positive actions and behaviors in your dog.

4. Be the Protector - To keep your dog relaxed and confident, always let your dog know that you are the protector. Their job is only to alert you, and then you take over to protect your territory.

5. Everything on Your Terms - Although we can welcome those sweet faces and the occasional play, as the head of the family everything must happen on your terms. You initiate play time, meal time, grooming and walks.

6. Walking Builds Bonds - Walking is one of the best bonding activities you can do with your dog. Ideally your walks should be loose leash. If they pull, stop and turn the walk in the other direction.

7. Remain Consistent - It is important to remain consistent with your behavior and with the behavior you expect from your dog. Everyone in the house should be on the same page and keep all training with your dog consistent.

The Furry Family Coach
Jessica L. Fisher is

CANINE COMMANDMENTS

<u>Positivity</u> – Always remain calm and positive with your dog. Your energy determines their behavior. Remain calm and positive and they will too!

<u>Patience</u> – You and your dog speak different languages. Be patient, take your time, take breaks, try again.

<u>Shape Your Dogs Behaviors</u> – Use food and other high value objects to shape positive actions and behaviors in your dog.

<u>Be the Protector</u> – To keep your dog relaxed and confident, always let your dog know that you are the protector. Their job is only to alert you, and then you take over to protect your territory.

<u>Everything on your Terms</u> – Although we can welcome those sweet faces and the occasional play, as the head of the family everything must happen on your terms. You initiate play time, meal time, grooming, walks, etc.

<u>Walking Builds Bonds</u> – Walking is one of the best bonding activities you can do with your dog. Ideally your walks should be loose leash. If they pull, stop and turn the walk in the other direction.

<u>Remain Consistent</u> – It is important to remain consistent with your behavior and with the behavior you expect from your dog. Everyone in the house should be on the same page and keep all training with your dog consistent.

Made in the USA
Columbia, SC
09 June 2019